Microsoft Forms

The Microsoft 365 Companion Series

Dr. Patrick Jones

OLYMPUS ACADEMY
PRESS

TABLE OF CONTENTS

MICROSOFT FORMS: SIMPLIFY SURVEYS, STREAMLINE FEEDBACK

In a world driven by data and insights, gathering information efficiently and effectively is more important than ever. Whether you're an educator seeking feedback from students, a business owner conducting market research, or a team leader evaluating a project's success, having the right tool to collect, analyze, and act on data is essential.

Enter Microsoft Forms, a versatile, user-friendly solution designed to simplify the process of creating surveys, quizzes, and polls. Part of the Microsoft 365 suite, Forms is a powerful yet accessible application that allows you to engage your audience, gather insights, and make data-driven decisions—all without the need for advanced technical skills.

This book is your guide to mastering Microsoft Forms, exploring its features, and leveraging its potential to transform the way you gather and utilize information. Whether you're new to Forms or looking to unlock its hidden capabilities, you'll find practical advice, relatable examples, and actionable tips to make your learning journey both educational and enjoyable.

While creating surveys or collecting data might seem straightforward, doing it effectively requires more than just asking questions. It's about designing forms that engage respondents, collecting data that's easy to analyze, and ensuring the process is efficient for both you and your audience.

This book aims to:

- Demystify Microsoft Forms and its capabilities.
- Provide practical guidance on designing impactful forms.

- Explore how Forms integrates with other Microsoft 365 tools like Excel, Teams, and SharePoint.

- Highlight advanced features, including automation and AI-powered insights.

As you progress through these chapters, you'll gain the confidence and skills to use Forms in innovative and effective ways, no matter your field or goals.

Microsoft Forms stands out for its simplicity. Unlike some survey tools that require steep learning curves or complex setups, Forms is designed to be intuitive. With just a few clicks, you can create a professional-looking survey or quiz that's ready to distribute. Yet beneath its straightforward interface lies a wealth of powerful features that can elevate your data collection efforts.

Imagine being able to:

- Create a training feedback form that automatically compiles results into a detailed report.

- Design a customer satisfaction survey that syncs with Teams to share real-time insights.

- Build a quiz that grades itself, saving hours of manual effort.

This is the power of Microsoft Forms—simplicity combined with functionality.

This book is structured to guide you from the basics to advanced features, providing a comprehensive understanding of Microsoft Forms. Here's what you can expect:

1. **What Is Microsoft Forms?** Learn about the core features, capabilities, and role of Forms within the Microsoft 365 ecosystem.

2. **Why Use Microsoft Forms?** Discover the benefits of using Forms, including its ease of use, versatility, and integration with other tools.

3. **Getting Started with Microsoft Forms:** Step-by-step instructions to create your first form or quiz, customize its settings, and share it with respondents.

4. **Best Practices:** Explore strategies for designing effective forms, from crafting clear questions to ensuring accessibility.

5. **Tips and Tricks:** Unlock hidden features, time-saving shortcuts, and advanced options to maximize efficiency.

6. **Copilot in Microsoft Forms:** See how AI-driven tools like Microsoft Copilot can enhance your data collection and analysis process.

7. **Common Pitfalls:** Avoid common mistakes that can undermine your forms' effectiveness, and learn how to overcome challenges.

8. **Episode Example:** Follow Sarah's journey as she uses Microsoft Forms to gather critical feedback, showcasing its features in action.

9. **Summary and Reflection:** Recap the key lessons and reflect on how Sarah's experience mirrors your own learning journey.

10. **Final Thoughts:** Conclude with insights on how Forms fits into the larger Microsoft 365 ecosystem and encourage further exploration.

Throughout this book, you'll follow the story of Sarah, a project manager tasked with improving her team's workflows. Sarah discovers Microsoft Forms while looking for a way to gather feedback efficiently. From her initial hesitation to her ultimate success, Sarah's journey illustrates how Forms can simplify complex tasks and deliver impactful results.

Her story isn't just a case study—it's a mirror of your own potential to learn, grow, and transform the way you work.

Microsoft Forms is more than a survey tool—it's a gateway to smarter data collection, streamlined processes, and actionable insights. As you delve into the next chapter, "What Is Microsoft Forms?", you'll gain a deeper understanding of its capabilities and why it's a must-have tool for anyone looking to simplify and optimize their workflows.

Let's begin this exciting journey together and unlock the full potential of Microsoft Forms!

WHAT IS MICROSOFT FORMS?

Microsoft Forms is an intuitive, user-friendly application designed to simplify the process of collecting and analyzing data. Whether you're creating surveys, quizzes, polls, or feedback forms, Microsoft Forms makes it easy to design, distribute, and gather insights—all within the secure Microsoft 365 ecosystem.

At its core, Forms is a digital tool for data collection. But it's more than that. It's a platform that empowers individuals and organizations to make informed decisions, streamline processes, and foster engagement. With its sleek interface, robust features, and seamless integration with other Microsoft apps, Forms is a versatile solution for anyone looking to gather and use information effectively.

At its simplest, Microsoft Forms allows you to create a form, share it with respondents, and view the results in real-time. Here's a quick overview of its core features:

1. **Create Forms Easily:** Build surveys, quizzes, and polls with a drag-and-drop interface. No coding or technical expertise is required.

2. **Customize Questions:** Choose from various question types, including multiple-choice, text, ratings, and more, to suit your needs.

3. **Share Seamlessly:** Distribute your forms via links, QR codes, or email, making it accessible to your audience on any device.

4. **Analyze Results Instantly:** View responses in real-time, generate charts, and export data to Excel for deeper analysis.

Microsoft Forms was introduced in 2016 as part of the Microsoft 365 suite. Initially designed as a lightweight survey tool for educators, it quickly gained popularity among businesses and individuals. Its evolution over the years has expanded its capabilities, transforming it into a robust platform for data collection across diverse use cases.

Forms is packed with features that make it a go-to tool for data collection:

1. **Variety of Question Types:**
   - **Multiple-Choice Questions:** Ideal for surveys and quizzes.
   - **Text Responses:** Gather detailed feedback or open-ended answers.
   - **Ratings and Likert Scales:** Measure satisfaction or opinions on a scale.
   - **Date and Ranking Options:** Collect dates or prioritize preferences easily.

2. **Customizable Design:**
   - Personalize your forms with themes, colors, and background images to make them visually appealing.
   - Add branding elements like logos for a professional touch.

3. **Real-Time Collaboration:**
   - Work with team members to design and edit forms collaboratively.
   - Share response data with stakeholders in real-time.

4. **Built-In Analytics:**
   - Automatically generate charts and graphs to visualize responses.
   - Identify trends and insights without the need for external tools.

5. **Integration with Microsoft 365:**

   o Use Excel to analyze response data in detail.

   o Share forms and results in Teams to foster collaboration.

   o Automate workflows with Power Automate for enhanced efficiency.

One of the standout advantages of Microsoft Forms is its seamless integration with the Microsoft 365 ecosystem. Forms isn't just a standalone app—it's a tool that works hand-in-hand with other apps to enhance your workflows.

- **Excel Integration:** Export responses directly to Excel for advanced data analysis.

- **Teams Collaboration:** Share forms and collect responses within Teams channels for streamlined communication.

- **Power Automate:** Automate form-related tasks, like sending email notifications when new responses are received.

- **SharePoint:** Store and manage form data securely in SharePoint, ensuring easy access and compliance.

Example: Imagine you're hosting a webinar and need attendee feedback. Using Forms, you can create a survey, share it via Teams, and export the responses to Excel for analysis—all within a single, integrated ecosystem.

The versatility of Microsoft Forms makes it suitable for a wide range of users:

1. **Educators:** Create quizzes, gather student feedback, or conduct virtual assessments.

2. **Businesses:** Run customer satisfaction surveys, collect employee feedback, or evaluate project outcomes.

3. **Nonprofits:** Engage donors, measure campaign effectiveness, or gather event RSVPs.

4. **Individuals:** Plan events, conduct polls, or collect RSVPs for personal projects.

Example: Sarah, a project manager, uses Forms to gather feedback from her team after completing a major project. This helps her identify areas for improvement and celebrate successes.

Forms is unique in its simplicity and accessibility. Unlike some survey tools that require a steep learning curve, Forms is designed to be intuitive, making it accessible to users of all skill levels.

Key Strengths:

- **Ease of Use:** You don't need to be tech-savvy to create and share forms.

- **Customizable:** Personalize forms to reflect your style or brand.

- **Real-Time Results:** View responses as they come in, allowing for immediate action.

- **Secure and Reliable:** Built within the Microsoft 365 ecosystem, Forms offers enterprise-grade security and compliance.

Pro Tip: Use Forms with a Microsoft 365 subscription for access to premium features, including higher response limits and advanced analytics.

Examples of Microsoft Forms in Action

1. **Education:** A teacher creates a quiz to assess student understanding, with auto-grading to save time.

2. **Business:** A marketing team conducts a customer satisfaction survey and uses the results to improve services.

3. **Personal Use:** An event organizer collects RSVPs and dietary preferences for a wedding using a custom form.

Now that you know what Microsoft Forms is and how it fits into the Microsoft 365 suite, the next step is understanding why you should use it.

WHY USE MICROSOFT FORMS?

In today's fast-paced world, the ability to gather and analyze information quickly and effectively is a critical skill. Whether you're an educator conducting assessments, a business professional seeking feedback, or an individual organizing an event, Microsoft Forms offers a powerful yet simple solution to streamline the process. But why choose Microsoft Forms over other tools?

This chapter explores the unique advantages of using Microsoft Forms, illustrating how it can transform the way you collect data, engage respondents, and drive decision-making. With its ease of use, versatility, and seamless integration within the Microsoft 365 ecosystem, Forms is more than just a survey tool—it's a game-changer for anyone who values efficiency and insight.

1. Simplicity Meets Power

One of the most compelling reasons to use Microsoft Forms is its balance of simplicity and functionality.

- **Intuitive Interface:** Forms is designed to be user-friendly, with a drag-and-drop interface that makes creating surveys, quizzes, and polls a breeze.
- **No Technical Expertise Required:** Whether you're a tech novice or a seasoned pro, Forms allows you to focus on your content, not the tool.

Example: Sarah, a team leader, created a feedback form for her colleagues in under 10 minutes, thanks to Forms' straightforward design.

Pro Tip: New to data collection? Start with a pre-built template to speed up the process and ensure a professional look.

2. Versatility Across Use Cases

Microsoft Forms isn't just for businesses or educators—it's a versatile tool that adapts to countless scenarios.

- **In Education:** Teachers can use Forms for quizzes, surveys, or attendance tracking. Auto-grading features make it easier to assess student progress.

- **In Business:** Teams can run customer satisfaction surveys, gather employee feedback, or evaluate training sessions.

- **For Personal Use:** Organize RSVPs for events, conduct family polls, or collect ideas for a community project.

Example: A nonprofit organization used Forms to gather feedback from donors after a fundraising event, enabling them to refine future campaigns.

Pro Tip: Combine Forms with Power Automate to trigger workflows, like sending thank-you emails after a response is submitted.

3. Real-Time Insights and Analytics

Forms offers built-in analytics to help you make sense of your data as it's collected.

- **Live Response Monitoring:** View responses in real-time, allowing for immediate action or adjustments.

- **Visual Data Representation:** Automatically generate charts and graphs for a quick overview of results.

- **Advanced Analysis:** Export data to Excel for deeper analysis and reporting.

Example: Sarah used the analytics dashboard to identify trends in her team's feedback, enabling her to address concerns before they escalated.

Pro Tip: Use conditional logic in Forms to tailor follow-up questions based on previous responses, making your data even more relevant.

4. Seamless Integration with Microsoft 365

Forms doesn't operate in isolation—it's designed to work seamlessly with the other tools in the Microsoft 365 suite.

- **Excel:** Export responses for detailed analysis or visualization.
- **Teams:** Share forms in a Teams channel to collect input directly from your team.
- **SharePoint:** Store and manage form data securely within your organization.
- **Power Automate:** Automate repetitive tasks, such as notifying stakeholders when a form is completed.

Example: A marketing team used Forms to collect customer feedback, linked it to Power Automate for real-time alerts, and analyzed the data in Excel to refine their strategy.

Pro Tip: Use Forms in Teams meetings to conduct live polls or gather audience input on the spot.

5. Accessibility and Inclusivity

Microsoft Forms is designed to be accessible to all users, ensuring inclusivity in data collection.

- **Mobile-Friendly Design:** Forms are optimized for mobile devices, allowing respondents to participate anywhere, anytime.
- **Multilingual Support:** Create forms in multiple languages to reach a broader audience.
- **Accessibility Features:** Built-in tools like screen reader compatibility and high-contrast modes ensure everyone can engage with your forms.

Example: Sarah created a multilingual customer satisfaction survey to cater to her company's diverse clientele, increasing response rates significantly.

6. Cost-Effective and Secure

For organizations already using Microsoft 365, Forms is included at no additional cost. It's a budget-friendly solution with enterprise-grade security.

- **No Extra Subscription Needed:** Forms is available to all Microsoft 365 users, from individuals to enterprises.

- **Data Security:** Responses are encrypted and stored securely within the Microsoft 365 environment.

- **Compliance:** Forms meets compliance standards for industries like healthcare and finance, ensuring data privacy.

Example: A healthcare provider used Forms to collect patient feedback securely, confident that their data complied with HIPAA regulations.

Pro Tip: If you need more advanced features, Forms Pro (now integrated into Microsoft Dynamics 365 Customer Voice) offers enhanced analytics and customization options.

7. Engaging and Interactive

Forms offers features to make surveys and quizzes more engaging, increasing response rates and participant satisfaction.

- **Branching Logic:** Customize the flow of questions based on respondents' answers.

- **Visual Customization:** Add images, videos, and branding elements to enhance the form's appeal.

- **Gamification:** Use quizzes with auto-grading to create fun, interactive experiences.

Example: A teacher used branching logic to create a math quiz that adapted based on the student's performance, offering personalized challenges.

Pro Tip: Add videos or images to explain questions more effectively, especially for complex topics.

8. Scalable for Any Audience

Whether you're collecting a handful of responses or thousands, Forms scales effortlessly to meet your needs.

- **High Response Limits:** Collect up to 50,000 responses per form in most plans, or more with premium options.
- **Cloud-Based Storage:** No need to worry about storage limits— data is securely stored in the cloud.
- **Global Reach:** Share your forms with anyone, anywhere, without restrictions.

Example: A global company used Forms to conduct an employee satisfaction survey across multiple offices, gathering thousands of responses without any technical hiccups.

9. Easy to Share and Distribute

Microsoft Forms provides multiple sharing options to reach your audience:

- **Public Links:** Share a link via email, social media, or messaging apps.
- **QR Codes:** Generate a QR code for quick access at events or on printed materials.
- **Embed Options:** Add your form to websites, blogs, or intranets.

Pro Tip: Use Forms' settings to control access, limiting responses to specific people or making it open to everyone.

Microsoft Forms offers a unique combination of simplicity, power, and integration, making it an indispensable tool for data collection. Whether you're gathering insights for a project, engaging with your audience, or streamlining your workflows, Forms provides the tools you need to succeed.

GETTING STARTED WITH MICROSOFT FORMS: YOUR FIRST STEPS

Microsoft Forms is designed to be user-friendly, making it easy to create your first survey, quiz, or poll in minutes. Whether you're collecting feedback, testing knowledge, or gathering opinions, this chapter will walk you through the basics of getting started. By the end, you'll be equipped to design a professional-looking form, customize it to suit your needs, and share it with your audience.

Step 1: Accessing Microsoft Forms

Before you start creating, you'll need to access Microsoft Forms. Here's how:

- **Via Browser:** Navigate to forms.office.com and sign in with your Microsoft 365 account.
- **In Teams:** Open Microsoft Teams, go to a channel, and add a Forms tab. This is ideal for team collaboration.
- **From Office.com:** On the Office homepage, select "Microsoft Forms" from the app launcher.

Pro Tip: Bookmark the Microsoft Forms webpage for quick access.

Step 2: Starting a New Form or Quiz

When you first open Microsoft Forms, you'll see two main options:

- **New Form:** Use this to create a survey, feedback form, or poll.
- **New Quiz:** Ideal for creating assessments or tests, with built-in grading features.

Example: Sarah, a project manager, chose "New Form" to gather feedback on her team's recent project.

Step 3: Designing Your Form

The heart of Microsoft Forms is its design interface. Here's how to create a form step-by-step:

1. **Add a Title and Description:**
   - Click on "Untitled Form" and enter a name that reflects your purpose, like "Customer Feedback Survey."
   - Add a short description to guide respondents, such as "We'd love your feedback on our new product!"

2. **Add Questions:**
   - Click "+ Add New" to choose a question type.
   - Options include multiple-choice, text, rating, date, and more.
   - Customize each question with options, hints, and required fields.

Pro Tip: Start with an open-ended question like "What do you think about our product?" to gather detailed feedback.

3. **Use Sections for Organization:**
   - Add sections to group related questions together, making the form easier to navigate.
   - Example: A customer satisfaction survey might have sections for "Product Feedback" and "Customer Service."

Step 4: Customizing the Look

Make your form visually appealing by customizing its appearance:

- **Themes:** Click the paintbrush icon to select a theme that matches your form's tone or branding.
- **Images and Videos:** Add visuals to make your form more engaging. For example, include a product image for context in a feedback form.
- **Branding:** If applicable, upload your organization's logo for a professional touch.

Pro Tip: Use high-quality images that are relevant to your form's content to increase respondent engagement.

Step 5: Setting Preferences

Tailor the form's settings to suit your needs:

- **Who Can Respond:** Decide if your form is open to anyone or restricted to specific people within your organization.
- **Response Options:** Limit each respondent to one submission or allow multiple responses.
- **Notification Settings:** Enable email notifications to stay informed about new responses.

Example: Sarah restricted her form to her team members and enabled notifications to review feedback in real-time.

Step 6: Previewing Your Form

Before sharing, preview your form to ensure everything looks and functions as intended.

- Click the Preview button in the toolbar.
- View the form as both a desktop and mobile user to ensure it's optimized for all devices.

Pro Tip: Test the form yourself or send it to a colleague for a second opinion before distributing it widely.

Step 7: Sharing Your Form

Microsoft Forms provides multiple sharing options to reach your audience:

- **Copy Link:** Generate a unique URL to share via email, social media, or messaging apps.

- **QR Code:** Perfect for printed materials like flyers or event programs.

- **Embed Code:** Integrate your form into websites or intranets.

- **Email:** Use the built-in email option to send invitations directly to respondents.

Example: Sarah shared her form via Teams, ensuring her team could access it seamlessly.

Pro Tip: Use the "Shorten URL" option to make links easier to share and remember.

Step 8: Viewing and Analyzing Responses

Once responses start rolling in, Forms makes it easy to monitor and analyze them:

- **Real-Time Results:** View responses as they come in through the Responses tab.

- **Charts and Graphs:** Automatically generated visuals provide an at-a-glance overview of trends.

- **Export to Excel:** For deeper analysis, export responses to Excel with a single click.

Example: Sarah used Excel to categorize her team's feedback into actionable insights, helping her identify areas for improvement.

Step 9: Using Templates for Efficiency

If you're short on time or need inspiration, Forms offers pre-built templates for common use cases:

- Customer feedback
- Event registrations
- Employee surveys
- Quizzes and assessments

Pro Tip: Customize templates to suit your specific needs, saving time while ensuring professionalism.

Step 10: Experimenting with Advanced Features

Once you're comfortable with the basics, explore Forms' advanced capabilities:

- **Branching Logic:** Customize the flow of questions based on previous responses.
- **Progress Indicators:** Enable progress bars to give respondents a sense of completion.
- **Custom Thank-You Messages:** Add a personalized message to thank respondents after submission.

Example: Sarah used branching logic to direct her team to different follow-up questions based on their role in the project.

Congratulations! You've taken the first steps toward mastering Microsoft Forms. By following this guide, you've learned how to access Forms, create a customized survey or quiz, and share it with your audience.

BEST PRACTICES FOR USING MICROSOFT FORMS

Creating a Microsoft Form is simple, but designing a form that's effective, engaging, and insightful requires strategy. Whether you're gathering feedback, conducting surveys, or creating quizzes, following best practices ensures that your forms are clear, professional, and yield actionable results.

This chapter explores tried-and-true techniques to help you make the most of Microsoft Forms, from crafting impactful questions to optimizing the user experience. By adopting these best practices, you'll maximize the value of your data collection efforts while keeping your respondents engaged.

1. Define Your Purpose Clearly

The Best Practice: Start with a clear goal in mind. What do you want to achieve with your form? Whether it's collecting feedback, testing knowledge, or conducting a survey, having a well-defined purpose will guide your design process.

- **Example:** Sarah wanted to gather feedback on a recent team project. Her goal was to identify strengths and areas for improvement, so she focused her questions on those topics.
- Avoid unnecessary questions that don't align with your objective.

Pro Tip: Write down your goal in one sentence before starting your form, and refer back to it as you build your questions.

2. Keep It Simple and Focused

The Best Practice: Simplicity is key. Overloading your form with too many questions or complex wording can overwhelm respondents and lead to incomplete submissions.

- Use straightforward language that is easy to understand.
- Limit the number of questions to what's essential.

Example: Sarah kept her project feedback form under 10 questions, ensuring it could be completed in under five minutes.

Pro Tip: For longer forms, use sections to break up content into manageable chunks.

3. Craft Engaging and Clear Questions

The Best Practice: Your questions are the heart of your form. Make sure they're well-written, engaging, and designed to elicit meaningful responses.

- Use open-ended questions sparingly; they're valuable but can be time-consuming for respondents.
- Be specific. For example, instead of "How was your experience?", ask "How would you rate your experience with our customer service?"
- Avoid leading questions that bias the response.

Pro Tip: Use a mix of question types (e.g., multiple-choice, Likert scale, text) to keep the form engaging and accommodate different preferences.

4. Optimize the Flow of Questions

The Best Practice: Arrange your questions logically, leading respondents through the form in a natural progression.

- Begin with easy, non-intrusive questions to build comfort.
- Group related questions together under sections or headings.

- Use branching logic to skip irrelevant questions based on prior answers.

Example: Sarah used branching logic to direct team members to different questions depending on their role in the project.

Pro Tip: Preview your form to ensure the flow makes sense before sharing it.

5. Personalize Where Possible

The Best Practice: Personalization helps respondents feel valued and increases engagement.

- Include a personalized introduction or thank-you message.
- Add branding elements like your company's logo or a color scheme that reflects your organization.

Example: Sarah added her team's logo to the feedback form and included a thank-you note in the closing message.

Pro Tip: Use the customization options in Forms to match your organization's branding for a professional touch.

6. Test Your Form Before Sharing

The Best Practice: Always test your form to catch errors, improve usability, and ensure everything works as intended.

- Complete the form yourself to experience it from the respondent's perspective.
- Share it with a colleague for feedback on clarity and design.

Example: Sarah tested her form with a teammate, who suggested rephrasing a confusing question for better clarity.

Pro Tip: Use Forms' preview mode to view your form on both desktop and mobile devices.

7. Make It Accessible

The Best Practice: Ensure your form is inclusive and accessible to all users, including those with disabilities.

- Use high-contrast colors and readable fonts.

- Add alt text for any images or visuals.

- Run Microsoft Forms' built-in accessibility checker to identify potential issues.

Pro Tip: Avoid relying on color alone to convey meaning; add text labels or patterns for clarity.

8. Respect Respondents' Time

The Best Practice: Keep your form concise and respect the time of your respondents.

- Include a progress indicator for longer forms to manage expectations.

- Pre-fill questions where possible (e.g., respondent name or email) if you have the data.

Example: Sarah's feedback form included only questions relevant to each respondent's role, saving time and increasing completion rates.

Pro Tip: Mention the estimated time to complete the form in your introduction to set clear expectations.

9. Protect Data and Privacy

The Best Practice: Build trust with your respondents by safeguarding their data.

- Use Forms' settings to control access, such as limiting responses to specific individuals or requiring sign-ins.

- Clearly state how the collected data will be used.

Example: Sarah included a note in her form's introduction explaining that feedback would be anonymized to encourage honest responses.

Pro Tip: Enable encryption settings for sensitive forms, such as those collecting personal or financial information.

10. Analyze Responses Effectively

The Best Practice: Ensure your form is set up to provide actionable insights from responses.

- Use clear, measurable questions to generate meaningful data.
- Leverage Forms' built-in analytics for quick overviews and trends.
- Export data to Excel for deeper analysis if needed.

Example: After her team submitted feedback, Sarah used Forms' analytics dashboard to create a presentation summarizing the results.

Pro Tip: Filter responses in Excel to focus on specific groups or trends, such as feedback from team leads or junior members.

By following these best practices, you can create forms that are not only effective but also engaging and respectful of your respondents' time. The result? Higher response rates, better data quality, and more meaningful insights.

TIPS AND TRICKS FOR MASTERING MICROSOFT FORMS

Microsoft Forms is packed with powerful features and hidden gems that can save you time, improve your forms' effectiveness, and elevate your data collection process. Whether you're a beginner or an experienced user, this chapter provides actionable tips and tricks to help you get the most out of Forms.

From enhancing your design to automating workflows, these practical insights will unlock the full potential of this versatile tool, ensuring your forms stand out and deliver impactful results.

1. Use Templates to Save Time

The Trick: Microsoft Forms offers a range of pre-built templates for common use cases, such as feedback surveys, quizzes, and event registrations.

- **Where to Find Them:** On the Forms homepage, browse the template gallery to find a starting point for your form.
- **Customize Templates:** Tailor the questions, design, and settings to match your needs.

Pro Tip: If you frequently create similar forms, save one as a template to reuse later.

2. Explore the Power of Branching Logic

The Trick: Make your forms dynamic and personalized by using branching logic to display specific questions based on respondents' answers.

- **How to Use It:**

- o   Select a question, click the three-dot menu, and choose "Add Branching."

- o   Define which questions appear based on the respondent's selection.

- **Example:** In a customer satisfaction survey, show follow-up questions only to respondents who rate their experience as "poor."

Pro Tip: Plan your questions in advance to ensure a smooth flow for all respondents.

3. Enhance Engagement with Visuals

The Trick: Adding images, videos, or GIFs can make your forms more engaging and visually appealing.

- **How to Add Visuals:**

  - o   Click the image or video icon within a question to upload media.

  - o   Use visuals to clarify complex questions or add a personal touch.

- **Example:** A teacher included an image of a math problem to help students visualize the question.

Pro Tip: Use high-quality visuals that are relevant and don't distract from the main content.

4. Take Advantage of the Mobile-Friendly Design

The Trick: Microsoft Forms is optimized for mobile devices, ensuring your forms look great and are easy to complete on any screen size.

- Test your form on a mobile device to ensure it's user-friendly.

- Use concise questions and avoid long text blocks for better readability on smaller screens.

Pro Tip: QR codes are a great way to share mobile-friendly forms quickly at events or meetings.

5. Add a Progress Bar for Longer Forms

The Trick: For forms with multiple sections, enable the progress bar to let respondents know how far along they are.

- **How to Enable It:** Go to "Settings" and check the "Progress Bar" option.
- **Why It Helps:** Progress bars reduce form abandonment by setting clear expectations for respondents.

Pro Tip: Use concise sections and keep each one focused on a specific topic to maintain engagement.

6. Customize the Thank-You Message

The Trick: Personalize the post-submission thank-you message to leave a lasting impression or provide next steps.

- **How to Edit It:** In the Settings menu, customize the text that respondents see after completing the form.
- **Example:** "Thank you for your feedback! We'll use your input to improve our services."

Pro Tip: Include a link to another form, website, or survey to guide respondents further.

7. Automate Workflows with Power Automate

The Trick: Connect Microsoft Forms with Power Automate to streamline repetitive tasks.

- **Examples of Automation:**
    - Send an email notification when a new response is submitted.
    - Save responses to a SharePoint list or Excel file automatically.
    - Create tasks in Microsoft Planner based on form submissions.
- **How to Set It Up:** Use Power Automate templates or create custom workflows to integrate Forms with other apps.

Pro Tip: Test your workflow with sample data to ensure it works as intended.

8. Secure Sensitive Data

The Trick: Use Forms' privacy and security settings to protect sensitive information.

- **How to Restrict Access:**
    - Limit responses to people within your organization.
    - Require sign-ins for added security.
- **Encryption:** All data is encrypted, but you can add password protection for extra peace of mind.

Pro Tip: Use clear disclaimers to inform respondents how their data will be used.

9. Export Data for Deeper Analysis

The Trick: Forms makes it easy to export responses to Excel for more advanced analysis.

- **How to Export:**

- o Click the "Responses" tab, then "Open in Excel."

- o Use Excel to filter, sort, and visualize your data.

- **Example:** Sarah exported her survey results to create a pivot chart summarizing trends.

Pro Tip: Use Excel formulas or Power BI for advanced insights and reporting.

10. Collaborate in Real-Time

The Trick: Work with your team to create and edit forms collaboratively.

- **How to Collaborate:**
  - o Click the three-dot menu and select "Collaborate or Duplicate."
  - o Share the collaboration link with your team members.
- **Example:** Sarah and her colleague worked together to refine questions for their team feedback form.

Pro Tip: Assign roles and responsibilities to avoid overlapping edits.

11. Use Multiple Sharing Options

The Trick: Microsoft Forms offers flexible sharing methods to reach your audience.

- **Options Include:**
  - o Sharing a link via email or chat.
  - o Embedding the form on a website.
  - o Generating a QR code for in-person events.
- **Example:** Sarah shared her survey link in a Teams chat, ensuring quick access for her team.

Pro Tip: Use the "Shorten URL" option to make links more manageable and professional.

12. Keep Learning and Experimenting

The Trick: Microsoft Forms regularly updates with new features and capabilities. Stay curious and keep experimenting to discover new ways to use the tool.

- **Where to Learn More:**
    - Explore Microsoft's official documentation and tutorials.
    - Join forums and communities to exchange tips with other users.

Pro Tip: Keep an eye on AI-powered enhancements, such as improved analytics and automation features, to stay ahead of the curve.

These tips and tricks will help you unlock the full potential of Microsoft Forms, turning a simple survey tool into a powerful data collection platform. By experimenting with these features and integrating them into your workflow, you'll create forms that are not only efficient but also engaging and impactful.

REVOLUTIONIZING DATA COLLECTION WITH AI

Imagine having an intelligent assistant by your side as you create surveys, quizzes, and feedback forms. That's exactly what Microsoft Copilot brings to Microsoft Forms—a powerful AI-driven tool that simplifies data collection, enhances analysis, and boosts efficiency.

Microsoft Copilot is not just about automating tasks; it's about elevating your form creation process to a new level of intelligence and adaptability. This chapter explores how Copilot works within Microsoft Forms, showcasing its features, practical use cases, and tips for maximizing its potential.

Microsoft Copilot leverages the power of AI to assist users in various Microsoft 365 applications, including Forms. With natural language processing (NLP), it understands your prompts and provides intelligent suggestions, making it an invaluable partner for designing and managing forms.

In Microsoft Forms, Copilot can:

- Generate form questions based on your input.

- Analyze response data to provide summaries and insights.

- Suggest improvements to your form structure or language.

Example: Sarah wanted to create a feedback form for her team but wasn't sure how to phrase her questions. With a simple prompt to Copilot—"Create a form to evaluate team performance"—she received a list of well-crafted questions in seconds.

How Copilot Enhances Microsoft Forms

1. **Smart Question Generation**

- The **Feature:** Copilot generates questions based on the context you provide, saving time and effort.

- **How It Works:** Simply describe your goal, such as "I need a customer satisfaction survey," and Copilot will suggest relevant questions.

- **Example:** Sarah asked Copilot to create a quiz for her training session. In moments, it provided a mix of multiple-choice and open-ended questions tailored to the session's content.

Pro Tip: Use clear and specific prompts for more accurate question suggestions.

2. **Response Analysis and Summarization**

- **The Feature:** Copilot analyzes responses to highlight trends, generate summaries, and identify key insights.

- **How It Works:** After collecting responses, ask Copilot to "Summarize the feedback" or "Highlight the top three concerns."

- **Example:** After her team completed the feedback form, Sarah used Copilot to identify recurring themes, such as better communication and more streamlined processes.

Pro Tip: Combine Copilot's insights with Excel or Power BI for deeper data visualization.

3. **Improved Question Clarity**

- **The Feature:** Copilot reviews your form for clarity and suggests rephrasing confusing or ambiguous questions.

- How It Works: Enter a command like "Make my questions easier to understand," and Copilot will provide rewritten suggestions.
- Example: Sarah's question, "How was your experience?" was rephrased by Copilot to "How satisfied were you with your experience today?" for better specificity.

Pro Tip: Use this feature to ensure your form resonates with diverse audiences.

4. **Tailored Themes and Branding**
   - The Feature: Copilot suggests design themes that align with your form's purpose or audience.
   - How It Works: Prompt Copilot with something like "Add a professional theme for a corporate survey," and it will select appropriate styles and colors.
   - Example: Sarah's form for her client meeting was automatically customized with her company's logo and brand colors.

Pro Tip: Preview Copilot's design choices and tweak them to fit your specific preferences.

5. **Advanced Automation with Power Automate**
   - The Feature: Copilot integrates with Power Automate to suggest workflows for managing responses.
   - How It Works: Describe your automation needs, such as "Send an email summary after a form is submitted," and Copilot will build the workflow for you.

- o **Example:** Sarah used Copilot to automate a process where each form submission triggered an email alert to her manager.

Pro Tip: Experiment with complex workflows, like routing responses to different teams based on keywords.

Practical Use Cases for Copilot in Microsoft Forms

- **Education:** Create auto-grading quizzes with Copilot's question generation and insights.

- **Business:** Automate response handling, such as routing customer feedback to the relevant department.

- **Events:** Use Copilot to craft registration forms and analyze attendee preferences.

- **Personal Projects:** Build engaging polls or surveys with visually appealing themes.

Example: Sarah hosted a virtual event and used Copilot to craft a post-event survey that included tailored follow-up questions based on attendee feedback.

Tips for Using Copilot Effectively

1. **Be Specific with Prompts:** The clearer your input, the more relevant Copilot's suggestions will be.

2. **Iterate on Suggestions:** Use Copilot's output as a starting point and refine it to suit your needs.

3. **Explore Integrations:** Combine Copilot with Excel, Power Automate, and other Microsoft tools for advanced functionality.

4. **Test Before Sharing:** Always preview and test forms generated with Copilot to ensure they align with your goals.

Pro Tip: Treat Copilot as a collaborator, not a replacement. Your input and expertise ensure the final product meets your expectations.

As Microsoft continues to enhance its AI capabilities, Copilot's role in Microsoft Forms will only grow. Future updates may include deeper contextual understanding, more advanced analytics, and even predictive modeling based on response data.

By embracing Copilot, you're not just improving your current workflow—you're future-proofing your approach to data collection and analysis.

Microsoft Copilot in Forms offers a glimpse into the future of intelligent data collection, where AI enhances your ability to gather insights and make informed decisions. In the next chapter, "Common Pitfalls When Using Microsoft Forms," we'll explore challenges users often face and provide strategies to overcome them. Let's ensure your journey with Forms continues to be smooth and successful!

COMMON PITFALLS AND HOW TO AVOID THEM

Microsoft Forms is a powerful and intuitive tool, but even the best tools can present challenges if not used effectively. Whether it's miscommunicating with your audience, mismanaging responses, or overlooking critical features, small mistakes can lead to big headaches. The good news? These pitfalls are easy to avoid once you know what to watch for.

In this chapter, we'll explore common mistakes users encounter when using Microsoft Forms and provide actionable strategies to overcome them. By recognizing these challenges ahead of time, you can create forms that are not only efficient but also impactful.

1. Overloading Your Form with Questions

The Pitfall:
Too many questions can overwhelm respondents, leading to incomplete submissions or rushed answers.

Why It Happens:
Users often feel compelled to cover every possible angle, resulting in lengthy forms.

How to Avoid It:

- Define your objective before you start. Only include questions that align directly with your goal.

- Group related questions into sections to make the form feel more manageable.

- Use branching logic to show follow-up questions only when necessary.

Example: Sarah initially created a 25-question feedback form but trimmed it down to 10 focused questions after realizing most were redundant.

2. Using Ambiguous or Vague Questions

The Pitfall:
Poorly worded questions can confuse respondents, resulting in unclear or inaccurate answers.

Why It Happens:
Users often write questions quickly without considering how they'll be interpreted.

How to Avoid It:

- Be specific. Instead of asking, "Did you like it?" ask, "How satisfied were you with the service provided?"

- Use examples or context if necessary, such as "On a scale of 1 to 5, how likely are you to recommend our product to a friend?"

- Test your form by asking a colleague to review the questions for clarity.

Pro Tip: Microsoft Copilot can suggest clearer phrasing for ambiguous questions.

3. Ignoring the Audience's Perspective

The Pitfall:
Failing to consider the needs and preferences of your respondents can lead to low engagement or irrelevant responses.

Why It Happens:
Form creators sometimes design forms based on their own perspective rather than the respondent's.

How to Avoid It:

- Put yourself in the respondent's shoes. What information do they need to answer effectively?

- Tailor your language and tone to your audience. For example, use formal language for professional surveys and casual language for informal polls.

Example: Sarah adjusted her feedback form's tone to be more conversational when surveying her team, making it feel less formal and more engaging.

4. Overlooking Accessibility

The Pitfall:
Not optimizing your form for accessibility can exclude respondents with disabilities.

Why It Happens:
Accessibility features are often overlooked in the rush to complete a form.

How to Avoid It:

- Use Forms' accessibility checker to identify and address issues.

- Provide alt text for images and use high-contrast themes.

- Avoid relying solely on color to convey meaning; include labels or patterns.

Pro Tip: Always test your form with accessibility tools to ensure inclusivity.

5. Neglecting Response Management

The Pitfall:
Failing to plan how you'll manage and analyze responses can make it harder to extract meaningful insights.

Why It Happens:
Users often focus on form creation but don't think about how they'll handle the data afterward.

How to Avoid It:

- Use Microsoft Forms' built-in analytics for quick insights.

- Export responses to Excel for advanced analysis and visualization.

- Plan ahead for how you'll organize and store response data, especially for large-scale surveys.

Example: Sarah used Power Automate to categorize responses into folders based on department, saving hours of manual work.

6. Not Testing the Form Before Sharing

The Pitfall:
Sharing a form with errors or poor design can frustrate respondents and reduce completion rates.

Why It Happens:
Users often skip testing due to time constraints or overconfidence in their design.

How to Avoid It:

- Always preview your form on multiple devices, including mobile phones.

- Ask a colleague to complete the form and provide feedback.

- Test branching logic and conditional questions to ensure they work as intended.

Pro Tip: Look for typos, broken links, or confusing instructions during testing.

7. Failing to Personalize the Experience

The Pitfall:
Generic, impersonal forms can feel cold and disengaging, reducing respondent motivation.

Why It Happens:
Form creators may prioritize speed over personalization.

How to Avoid It:

- Add a welcoming introduction and a personalized thank-you message.

- Use branding elements like logos and themes that reflect your organization.

- Tailor questions to the audience's specific interests or experiences.

Example: Sarah added her company logo and a personalized thank-you note to her customer satisfaction survey, increasing response rates by 20%.

8. Forgetting to Secure Sensitive Data

The Pitfall:
Neglecting to enable proper security settings can lead to unauthorized access or data breaches.

Why It Happens:
Users may not fully understand Forms' security features or fail to prioritize them.

How to Avoid It:

- Restrict access to specific people or groups when needed.

- Use encrypted connections for sensitive information.

- Provide a disclaimer about how respondent data will be used and stored.

Pro Tip: Use password protection for forms collecting confidential information.

9. Overcomplicating the Design

The Pitfall:
Overloading your form with too many visuals, fonts, or colors can make it look cluttered and unprofessional.

Why It Happens:
Users often try to make forms visually appealing but overdo it.

How to Avoid It:

- Stick to a consistent color scheme and font style.

- Use visuals sparingly and only when they enhance understanding.

- Choose clean, minimalistic themes that focus attention on the content.

Example: Sarah simplified her event registration form by removing unnecessary graphics, making it easier to navigate.

10. Misusing Copilot Suggestions

The Pitfall:
Relying too heavily on Copilot's suggestions without tailoring them can result in generic or irrelevant forms.

Why It Happens:
Users may assume Copilot's output is perfect without reviewing or refining it.

How to Avoid It:

- Treat Copilot as a starting point, not a final solution.

- Edit and personalize suggestions to align with your specific needs and audience.

Pro Tip: Use Copilot's insights as inspiration but add your expertise to create truly impactful forms.

By avoiding these common pitfalls, you can create forms that are efficient, engaging, and effective. Whether you're designing a simple survey or a complex quiz, a thoughtful approach will ensure you gather the insights you need without frustrating your respondents.

SARAH'S MICROSOFT FORMS SUCCESS STORY

Sarah sat at her desk, feeling a mix of anticipation and uncertainty. She had been tasked with organizing her company's annual team feedback survey—a critical tool for evaluating team satisfaction and identifying areas for improvement. While she had used Microsoft Forms sparingly in the past, this was the first time she would create and manage a form of such importance.

Her mind buzzed with questions: How would she ensure the survey gathered meaningful insights? What if respondents didn't take it seriously? Determined to rise to the challenge, Sarah decided it was time to fully explore the capabilities of Microsoft Forms.

Sarah began by reflecting on the purpose of the survey. She wanted to understand how her team felt about their current work environment, communication dynamics, and opportunities for growth. She jotted down her objectives:

1. Identify what the team values most about their work experience.

2. Highlight pain points that need addressing.

3. Gather suggestions for future improvements.

With her goals clearly defined, she opened Microsoft Forms and started a new form titled "Annual Team Feedback Survey."

Sarah knew that keeping the survey simple and engaging was key. Drawing on what she'd learned about best practices, she broke the form into three sections:

1. **Work Environment:** Questions focused on overall satisfaction, tools provided, and workload balance.

2. **Communication:** A section addressing team dynamics, clarity of instructions, and leadership accessibility.

3. **Growth Opportunities:** Queries about training, career development, and mentorship.

For each section, she added a mix of question types:

- Multiple-choice for quick, quantifiable responses.
- Text fields for open-ended feedback.
- A rating scale to gauge satisfaction levels.

To make the survey visually appealing, she selected a theme with calming blue tones and uploaded her company's logo.

As Sarah crafted her questions, she felt unsure about some of the phrasing. She decided to enlist the help of Microsoft Copilot, typing the prompt:
"Create questions for a team satisfaction survey focusing on communication and growth."

Within seconds, Copilot suggested:

- "How would you rate the quality of communication within your team?"
- "What opportunities for professional growth have been most beneficial to you?"
- "What improvements would you suggest for better leadership support?"

Impressed with the suggestions, Sarah integrated them into her form, tweaking the wording to match her tone.

Copilot's question generation saved Sarah time and gave her inspiration for additional topics she might have missed.

Sarah wanted to ensure that the survey felt relevant to each respondent. She used branching logic to tailor questions based on the role of the team member.

For example:

- If a respondent selected "Team Lead" as their role, they were directed to questions about managing team dynamics.
- If they selected "Team Member," they received questions focused on collaboration and workload.

Testing the branching logic, Sarah smiled at how smoothly it worked. "This will keep the survey focused and engaging," she thought.

With the form complete, Sarah reviewed it on both desktop and mobile devices. Satisfied with the design and functionality, she clicked the "Share" button to generate a link.

She shared the survey link in her team's Microsoft Teams channel, adding a friendly message:
"Hi Team! Please take a few minutes to complete our annual feedback survey. Your input is invaluable in shaping our work environment. Responses are anonymous, and it should only take about 5 minutes. Thank you!"

As responses began rolling in, Sarah was excited to see the data take shape. Using the real-time analytics in Microsoft Forms, she noticed:

- High ratings for workload balance but lower scores for communication clarity.
- Recurring comments about the need for more one-on-one time with managers.
- Several team members suggested implementing mentorship programs.

Sarah exported the data to Excel for further analysis, using charts to visualize trends and identify actionable insights.

With the survey results summarized, Sarah presented her findings to leadership. She highlighted the team's appreciation for flexible workloads and proposed solutions for the communication challenges, including:

1. Bi-weekly team meetings to improve clarity and alignment.
2. A pilot mentorship program to foster growth and connection.

Leadership was impressed with her thorough analysis and actionable recommendations. "This survey has given us the clarity we needed to make meaningful changes," her manager said.

Sarah realized how far she'd come from feeling unsure about creating a survey to confidently delivering impactful insights. Microsoft Forms, with its intuitive design and advanced features, had transformed a daunting task into an achievable project.

Her experience taught her the value of starting with clear goals, using tools like Copilot to simplify the process, and keeping the respondent experience in mind.

Sarah's journey demonstrates the potential of Microsoft Forms to streamline data collection and uncover actionable insights. Whether you're conducting a survey, quiz, or feedback form, the principles she applied can guide your own success.

LEARNING FROM MICROSOFT FORMS

As we reach the end of this book, it's time to pause and reflect on the journey we've taken together. Microsoft Forms is far more than just a tool for creating surveys or quizzes—it's a gateway to efficient data collection, meaningful analysis, and impactful decision-making. From understanding its capabilities to exploring advanced features like Copilot and branching logic, you've gained the knowledge needed to turn ideas into actionable insights.

Let's summarize the key lessons from the book and take a moment to reflect on Sarah's journey, which mirrors the path you, as a reader, are on. Her story highlights how Microsoft Forms can transform a simple task into a meaningful opportunity for growth.

1. **Introduction to Microsoft Forms:** We started with an overview of Forms, exploring its role within the Microsoft 365 ecosystem and its potential to simplify data collection.

2. **What Is Microsoft Forms?:** This chapter provided a deep dive into the features and capabilities of Forms, showing how it integrates seamlessly with other tools like Excel, Teams, and SharePoint.

3. **Why Use Microsoft Forms?:** You discovered the unique advantages of Forms, from its intuitive design to its versatility across industries and use cases.

4. **Getting Started:** Practical steps guided you through creating your first form, customizing it, and sharing it with respondents.

5. **Best Practices:** We explored strategies for designing effective forms, crafting clear questions, and optimizing the user experience.

6. **Tips and Tricks:** This chapter revealed hidden features and shortcuts to enhance your productivity, from using templates to automating workflows.

7. **Copilot in Forms:** You learned how AI-driven features like question generation and response analysis can simplify and elevate your forms.

8. **Common Pitfalls:** We addressed challenges users often face and provided solutions to avoid them, ensuring a smooth and successful experience.

9. **Episode:** Sarah's story brought these lessons to life, illustrating how Forms can help overcome challenges and achieve impactful results.

Sarah's experience with Microsoft Forms is more than a story—it's a relatable example of how to approach learning and using new tools. Let's revisit her journey and draw parallels to your own:

- **Starting with Uncertainty:** Like many first-time users, Sarah felt unsure about where to begin. Her initial hesitation mirrors the common feeling of overwhelm when facing unfamiliar technology. But instead of giving up, she embraced the learning process, just as you have by reading this book.

- **Discovering the Power of Forms:** As Sarah explored Forms, she uncovered features that simplified her task, such as branching logic and Copilot's intelligent suggestions. Her excitement in learning these tools reflects the potential for growth and discovery in every reader's journey.

- **Applying Best Practices:** By keeping her survey focused and engaging, Sarah ensured meaningful responses from her team. Her thoughtful approach demonstrates the importance of applying best practices to achieve success.

- **Transforming Challenges into Opportunities:** Sarah's ability to analyze feedback and present actionable recommendations shows how Microsoft Forms can turn data into decisions.

Similarly, you now have the tools to use Forms for impactful outcomes in your own projects.

Sarah's story is a reminder that learning is a journey, and every step brings you closer to mastering new skills. Whether you're creating forms for work, education, or personal use, the lessons from her journey apply to yours.

This book has not only equipped you with technical knowledge but also encouraged a mindset of curiosity and adaptability. Microsoft Forms is a dynamic tool that evolves with your needs, and your willingness to explore its features ensures you'll always be prepared to meet new challenges.

Ask yourself:

- How has your understanding of Forms grown through this book?
- What features or strategies resonated with you the most?
- How will you apply what you've learned to achieve your goals?

While this book focused on Microsoft Forms, it's part of the larger Microsoft 365 ecosystem—a suite of tools designed to work together to enhance productivity and collaboration. Consider exploring:

- **SharePoint:** For organizing and managing form data.
- **Teams:** To collaborate on surveys and analyze results in real-time.
- **Excel:** For advanced data visualization and reporting.

The principles you've learned here—clear goals, thoughtful design, and leveraging AI—can be applied across Microsoft 365 tools, making your work more efficient and impactful.

Learning doesn't stop here. The digital world is constantly evolving, and tools like Microsoft Forms are continuously updated with new features and capabilities. Stay curious, keep experimenting, and embrace every opportunity to grow.

Your ability to adapt and innovate is your greatest strength. Whether you're creating your next form or exploring another Microsoft 365 tool, remember that every step forward brings new possibilities.

THE POWER OF FORMS AND THE MICROSOFT 365 ECOSYSTEM

As we close this book, take a moment to celebrate the progress you've made. You've not only explored the technical aspects of Microsoft Forms but also embraced its potential to transform the way you work, learn, and collaborate. What began as a simple tool for data collection has revealed itself to be a gateway to smarter workflows, deeper insights, and more meaningful connections.

This journey is about more than mastering Forms—it's about becoming more confident and capable in using technology to solve problems, inspire change, and make an impact.

Microsoft Forms is more than just a tool for surveys and quizzes; it's a platform for growth. With its intuitive design, powerful features, and seamless integration into the Microsoft 365 ecosystem, Forms enables you to:

- Collect meaningful data with ease.

- Make informed decisions based on real-time insights.

- Foster collaboration and communication across teams.

Think about Sarah's journey. What started as a challenge to create a simple feedback form grew into an opportunity to drive meaningful change within her organization. That's the power of Forms—not just as a tool, but as a catalyst for transformation.

Forms doesn't exist in isolation. It's part of a larger ecosystem designed to empower individuals and teams to achieve more. By exploring other Microsoft 365 tools, you'll uncover even more ways to enhance your workflows and accomplish your goals.

Consider how Forms integrates with:

- **Excel:** For advanced data analysis and visualization.

- **Teams:** To collaborate on forms, share results, and gather feedback in real-time.

- **SharePoint:** To store and organize responses securely.

- **Power Automate:** To automate workflows and save time.

Each tool complements the others, creating a cohesive experience where the whole is greater than the sum of its parts.

The beauty of technology is that it never stops evolving—and neither should you. Microsoft Forms, like the entire Microsoft 365 suite, is constantly updated with new features and capabilities. Staying curious and adaptable ensures you'll continue to grow and thrive in an ever-changing landscape.

- **Keep Learning:** Follow blogs, attend webinars, and explore tutorials to stay up to date on the latest features.

- **Experiment Fearlessly:** Try new tools, test different workflows, and push the boundaries of what you think is possible.

- **Teach Others:** Share your knowledge with colleagues, fostering a culture of learning and collaboration.

This book is just one step in your journey to mastering Microsoft 365. If you've enjoyed learning about Forms, consider exploring other tools in the *Microsoft 365 Companion Series*:

- **Microsoft SharePoint:** Organize, collaborate, and manage information like never before.

- **Microsoft OneDrive:** Simplify file storage and access across devices.

- **Microsoft Teams:** Revolutionize communication and teamwork in your organization.

- **Microsoft Copilot:** Unlock the full potential of AI-driven productivity.

Each book is designed to build on what you've learned here, equipping you with the skills and confidence to tackle new challenges.

Mastering a tool like Microsoft Forms is more than just a technical achievement—it's a mindset. It's about approaching challenges with curiosity, finding creative solutions, and embracing the tools that make your work and life easier.

As you move forward, remember that every form you create, every response you analyze, and every insight you gain is part of a larger journey of growth and transformation.

Thank you for letting this book be a part of your story. The next chapter is yours to write, and the possibilities are endless. Keep exploring, keep learning, and keep achieving.

Your ability to adapt, innovate, and grow is what will set you apart. Microsoft Forms is just one tool in your toolkit—but with the skills you've gained here, you're ready to tackle any challenge.

So go ahead: create, collaborate, and transform. The future is bright, and it's waiting for you to shape it.

www.ingramcontent.com/pod-product-compliance
Lightning Source LLC
LaVergne TN
LVHW052322060326
832902LV00023B/4542